BUILDING YOUR OWN STREET ROD
"Made Easy"

Dave Harvey

Published by:
Lulu.com

First published in 2007 by Lulu, Inc.

© Dave Harvey, 2007

ISBN number: 978-1-4303-0702-0

Printed and bound in the USA

INTRODUCTION

There are many references that apply to the E-Book

I'm Dave Harvey; you can call me Dave or Harv. I've been building street rods for others and myself for the past 23 years. During this time I've gained a lot of knowledge and experience that I'd like to pass onto you. I've built street rods out of both original steel cars and all new from the ground up with aftermarket parts, bodies, and chassis. Building a car is not as difficult as it seems. Once you start, you will realize this and wonder why you were ever afraid to try. That's normal. I was too! After waiting almost a year for a friend to paint my car, I decided to attempt it myself. For the money I would have paid him, I bought all the equipment and supplies to paint the car myself (a 1930 Ford 2 door). I started with a fender and found it wasn't that hard and was happy with the result. I had to do it twice to get down the technique, but it only took me a day. I'm not saying you should paint your own car, not everybody is set up to do it. I did it in a two-car garage at my home. My neighbors were cool and didn't mind or say anything to the city or authorities, otherwise I could've got in trouble. A good paint job can be had for around a thousand bucks, unless you have to have a well-known painter do it and that could cost upward to around $10,000. You can build a nice car for around $20–$35,000 using all the new merchandise available through street rod suppliers (I will give you all the resources you need to complete your car) unless you want big name paint and upholstery and that alone can cost up to $20,000 or more. Building an original car is more work and just as expensive if not more. I've done both many times and I've always preferred to build a glass car. You could just about build your entire car without leaving your house. With the resources I'm giving you, all you have to do is click away on the Internet with your mouse or use your phone and everything will be delivered to your doorstep. You wonder about registration well that's easy too. I'll walk you through it when the time comes. If you need help with anything or can't find a supplier close to you, I'll help you, email me and I will contact you within 48 hours. My email address is HarveyEnterprises@youbuildrod.com.

Remember, I'm a Dealer for Total Cost Involved, Wescott, and Heritage Hot Rods and can save you 15% off their list prices. You can visis my website at:
www.BuildingYourOwnStreetRod.com.

The information in this book is my own opinions and methods and meant to ease the building process for the would-be street rod builder.

The Links at the end of book lists resource phone numbers.

CONTENTS

INTRODUCTION 2

WHY BUILD YOUR OWN CAR 8

CHAPTER 1 – DECIDING ON A CAR 10

FIBERGLASS VS. STEEL 10

WHERE WILL I GET THE CAR 1

    BODY OPTIONS 13

        Original: 13

        After market metal bodies: 13

        After market fiberglass bodies: 14

    CHASSIS OPTIONS 16

CHAPTER 2 – PLANNING THE BUILD 19

WHERE WILL I BUILD THE CAR 19

WHAT PARTS DO I NEED TO BUY 21

    Chassis Parts 21

        Tires and wheels: 22

        Drive train: 22

    Body Parts 25

    Miscellaneous Parts 25

    Tools 27

        Hand tools: 27

Power tools and equipment:..2
Basic body working tools:...2

CHAPTER 3 – TIME TO ACT!................................2

ORDER THE STUFF..2

ORGANIZE THE STUFF.......................................3

LETS GO TO WORK..3
Fit the Body to the Frame...................................3
The Body..3
Doors and Trunk...3
Fenders Etc...3
Window Frames and Dash......................................3
Steering Column and Brake Pedal (after market car only)....3
Gas Tank (not the stock type) and Battery..................3
The Chassis...3
Register the Car..4
The Engine..4
The Transmission..4
Install the Engine and Transmission........................4
Finish the Engine...4
The Drive Shaft...4
Service the Fluids..4
Test Run the Engine...4

CHAPTER 4 – WORK THE BODY...............................4

BODYWORK, PREP PAINT AND PAINT..........................4

Having a Body and Paint Shop Do It................................48
Doing the Body Yourself................................48

CHAPTER 5 – ASSEMBLE CAR................................51

MOUNT THE BODY................................51
Front Fenders and Running Boards................................51
The Body and Rear Fenders................................51

CHAPTER 6 – WIRE THE CAR................................52

WIRE THE DASH................................52

WIRE THE BODY................................54

CHAPTER 7 – FINISH THE INTERIOR................................55

UPHOLSTERY (having it done at a shop)................................55

WINDOWS and MUFFLERS................................56

UPHOLSTERY (doing it yourself)................................58
Carpet................................59
Headliner................................60
Door and side panels................................61
Doors, Trunk Lid and Steering Column................................62

CHAPTER 8 - Checkout and Adjustment 64

Drive the Car 64

Adjustment 64

Finished at Last! 65

LINKS 65

PICTURE GALLERY 67

WHY BUILD YOUR OWN CAR

Chances are you're just like me, wanting to build your own car for the shear satisfaction of being able to say truthfully that you built it yourself. The satisfaction and feeling of accomplishment is enormous and one of the most rewarding experiences you will ever have. Also, it's rewarding and an investment, you will not lose money building a street rod. When you go to rod runs or car shows and listen to the participants talk you can get an idea of their pride. The ones that bought their car and never built one can't relate and they are

> I've always been able to sell the car for more than what it cost me to build it.

awkward trying to join some of the conversations. The ones who had their car built can sometimes fake it in a conversation depending on how involved they were in the building of it. Or, their just plain rich and it's just a toy to them. I built a car for a guy once who had money, but not enough to have one of the big boys build it. He came to me and got one for less than half the price. He had a Harley, a boat and now a street rod. The problem was he was not a hand's on guy and just wanted to have the toys so he could hang around those who were hands on, and when something went wrong, which is a normal occurrence, he was dead in the water. Fortunately most street rodders are helpful and friendly and came to his rescue. He told me he was unhappy because he couldn't just drive his car like a new production car and take it to the dealer for normal servicing. He could've brought it to me during the break in period, but he was a thousand miles away. I know you're not that way or you wouldn't be thinking about building a car.

Once you decide to build a car it becomes an adventure and it's not only exciting, but also fun and rewarding, all aspects of it, from the planning to the final shine on the paint job.

9

CHAPTER I – Deciding on a car

You probably already have a favorite car, but sometimes your favorite car may not be attainable so you need to look around and see what's available. Go to some rod runs and get some street rod magazines. Join the National Street Rod Association (NSRA) and they will send you Street Scene Magazine every month and it is loaded with all kinds of cars, events and street rod suppliers and dealers. Their web home page is http://www.nsra-usa.com. Phone: 901-452-4030

FIBERGLASS VS. STEEL

ONE IS STEEL ONE IS GLASS
WHICH IS WHICH

This is a big issue with a lot of street rodder's. I always hear "if it aint steel it aint real" and there are some serious debates about it, especially with the new after market metal body's available. An after market metal body is just as unreal as a fiberglass one in my book, so what's the big deal. So what if you get a glass body or a metal one. I prefer glass to metal any day for several reasons – It doesn't rust or dent; it's easy to repair or replace; it's lightweight; and it's relatively inexpensive.

From a building standpoint they are about the same procedure to build unless your going to do your own body work, prep work and paint. Then it's considerably more complicated. If you have the work done in a body/paint shop and there is minimal bodywork, the cost is about the same. When looking at resale value, the steel cars are slightly more expensive.

I used to try and tell which cars were steel or glass by running my fingers across the underside of the fender, glass always had a rough surface, but now the manufactures such as Down's in Michigan, are finishing the underside also. It's getting really hard to tell the difference any more. Neither can I tell by rapping my knuckle against the surface, they sound about the same to me. I suppose I ought to tell you though that my hearing is about half of what it used to be. If I used a ball peen hammer I could tell the difference when I heard the ping of steel, however I would probably eventually be caught and suffer an early demise at the hand's of the owner. There is one way to do it and that is to use a soft plastic or rubber coated magnet and touch it against the surface, but with my luck the metal would suck the magnet out of my hand and slam against the surface and cause a scratch or chip.

So who cares, it's a matter of preference and shouldn't be anyone's business except yours. I really do get irritated when someone knocks another's street rod. The real builders and old time rodder's will seldom talk bad about someone's car. My experience is that they show the same respect to all the rods and the ones who complain are the ones who had their car built or bought one already done and hardly ever touch a wrench. Always remember that street rodder's are very sensitive about their cars.

'32
ROADSTER

WHERE WILL I GET THE CAR

Now you need to decide where to look for your project car or
new body (we'll address chassis and other parts later). If it's
going to be a metal car you will have a choice between
an original car to make a project or to buy an after
market metal body. There are not a lot of choices when it
comes to an after market metal body. We'll look at metal and
glass separately. There are a wide range of glass body
dealers and lots of choices. If you want a car other than a
Ford, Willys or Chevy you will have to look for an original car
to make a project. I think there's a Mopar dealer or two.

Ok, I know what I want lets start looking.

If you're going to build a car from scratch you will need a real
title to register and title it. You can get this from a couple of
sources. Classic's (888) 870-8071, The Broadway Title Co.
www.broadwaytitle.com, Street Rod'n (410) 257-6522 (I've
used him, about $150 for a title).

BODY OPTIONS

RAW
BODY

Original:

A good place to start would be your local advertisements - newspaper, weekly free want ads, the Auto Trader magazine (the street rod addition), Street Scene magazine (NSRA) http://www.nsra-usa.com, Hemmings Motor News magazine http://www.hemmings.com, and eBay http://www.ebay.com. Email me and let me know what you're looking for and I'll help you.

After market metal bodies:

There are only a few after market metal body cars available. You can get a '28 or '32 roadster and a '32 3-window coupe at Brookville Roadsters in Brookville, OH http://www.brookville-roadster.com. Steve's Auto Restorations in Portland, OR has a '33/'34 ford roadster body, phone is 503-665-2222. Rodbods in Sparks, NV has a beautiful '32 roadster and you can see it at http://www.rodbodsusa.com. Lastly you can get the Dearborn Deuce '32 3-window coupe or '32 convertible roadster from Woodsy's Gearhead City in Philo, IL http://gearheadcity.com or from Hot Rods & Horsepower in Bradford, CN http://www.hotrodsandhorsepower.com.

After market fiberglass bodies:

Man, there are more body manufacture's than you can shake a stick at. I will give you the names of a few that I feel are the best quality at a reasonable price. I'm a Heritage Hot Rods and Wescott Bodies dealer and can save you 15%. I tried a couple of the other lower end dealers, I spent twice the time it normally takes to prep the car for paint and if you're having a shop do it for you it will cost you more than if you had bought the more expensive quality body. So here is a list you can consider:

Wescott's Auto Restyling in Boring, OR, Best Qulaity http://www.wescottsauto.com.

Poly Form Fiberglass in Watsonville, CA http://www.poli-form.com. Has a '27 Ford Roadster and '34 For 3-window coupe. Great quality.

Down's Manufacturing in Lawton, MI http://www.downsmfg.com. Has a wide variety of Fords and Chevy's. Great Quality, but not the best.

Redneck Street Rods in Atchison, KS http://www.redneckstreetrods.com. Has a '34 Ford coupe, '33 Ford sedan, '32 Ford 3-window coupe, '33 Ford cabster, and a '33 Plymouth 3-window coupe.

Heritage Hot Rods in Kankakee, IL http://www.heritagehotrods.com. This is in my opinion, the best buy for the money and I can save you 15% off the list price. Also, they have a good variety of bodies.

One of the things you will notice as you look at the body dealers is that most of them offer a rolling car. That means it comes with a chassis under it with tires and wheels on it, however, they are unusable and they are bolted to the axles only. The advertised chassis is usually bare bones. You can get it complete with everything installed, but the price is considerably more (between $3000 and $10000 depending on what options you get). One advantage to getting their rolling car is that the body comes bolted to the chassis. Seldom do bodies fit a chassis like a glove even though both are supposedly built to original factory specifications. Next we will look at chassis and their options.

CHASSIS OPTIONS

Dropped Axle

Quick Change

Above is a Total Cost Involved (TCI) deluxe '32 Ford chassis. It came with everything installed and included the polished Stainless steel, chrome and aluminum package with a Franklin quick-change rear end.

If you're building an original car into a street rod and want to use the original frame, you will have to box it in or reinforce it with steel plate. The original frames won't handle the torque and horsepower of the new motors. You also will need to upgrade the entire suspension with the same options offered with the new chassis. The first couple of cars I built I did this. I ran my own brake lines, boxed in the frame, made my own engine/transmission and rear end mounts, man I was really saving some bucks. However, the time I put in was enormous. When I started building cars for customers I couldn't afford to spend that much time so I ordered the complete chassis assemblies and guess what? There wasn't much difference in price at all. Then I started ordering the deluxe packages with chrome, stainless, and aluminum and guess what? It saved me countless hours in prep and painting of all the suspension parts. Now all I do is disassemble it when I get it home, take the frame to the powder coaters and have it coated and guess what? The powder coating cost about the same as the materials and prep supplies for paint and it doesn't cost me any of my time other than transporting it to and from the powder coaters. If your building a car for yourself and I suspect you are, you

16

might as well put out a little more cash and get the good stuff. Of course you don't want to go overboard, an independent dolled up Jag or Corvette rear end cost about $7000 more, which is fine if money is no object. On my most recent and last car I opted for the polished aluminum Currie rear end and it looks real nice. It was only a thousand more bucks. When you order a chassis you need to know the engine and transmission you're going to use. Also, it depends on the style of rod you're going to build. Super hi-tech you would probably want a hi-tech independent or pinched coil over front, conventional looks good with four bar suspension and nostalgia you'd want to consider an I-beam axle with hair pin suspension.

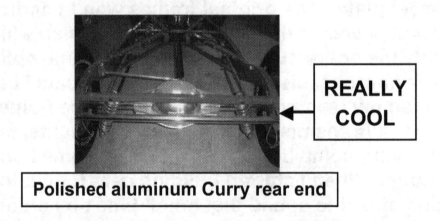

REALLY COOL ←

Polished aluminum Curry rear end

Hopefully I convinced you to buy a complete chassis, if not you will still have fun building it and save a little money while you're at it. Ok, lets see where to get the chassis and/or parts.

The first in the industry to build chassis was TCI (Total Cost Involved). They started as a partnership with Magnum Axle Company and broke up a couple of years after. They are the benchmark and the standard for the street rod industry. In the past 10 years there have been many other chassis manufacturers join the street rod industry and many of them have a great product. You can get all the parts you need to

17

complete your chassis or buy it already complete. It depends on your budget. Any way you look at it, it's not going to be cheap. The chassis above cost me around $8,000 less the tires, wheels and drive train and I am a TCI dealer. You're looking at about $10,000 retail. Most the dealers are pretty competitive in their prices. I've found that some of the 2nd party dealers have really good deals on chassis. I sell them at around 15% off. Look at Zig's Street Rods http://www.zigsstreetrods.com/zigs.html, they have really good deals also on TCI stuff with free shipping. If you're looking for something other than Ford, good luck!

TCI (Total Cost Involved) is located in Ontario, CA http://www.totalcostinvolved.com. Excellent service and quality products and I can sell you stuff over the Internet.

The Rod Factory is located in Phoenix, AZ, http://www.rodfactory.com has their own line of chassis and dealer for some of the other brands.

SO-CAL Speed Shop's main H.Q. is in Pomona, CA and have stores in OR, CO, NV, AZ, TX, and IL. http://so-calspeedshop.com. '32 and model "A" Ford chassis.

Down's Manufacturing in Lawton, MI http://www.downsmfg.com. Ford and Chevy chassis.

Lobeck's V8 Shop has two locations in OH, Cleveland 440-439-8143, and Springfield 937-325-8389. Has their own line of '33/'34 chassis.

After you have decided on the car and resources for your body and chassis you need to come up with a plan for the build.

CHAPTER 2 – Planning the Build

Here's a '32 Ford hi-boy I did in 1999

WHERE WILL I BUILD THE CAR

The first few cars I built were in Santa Maria, CA when we lived in a small 2-car garage house. Notice I said 2-car garage house instead of a 3-bedroom house. To be a street rodder you have to develop the jargon, we always think of a house in terms of garage space. I have a buddy named Vaughn who recently bought a really great garage with a beautiful house attached to it so his wife would be happy too! When you only have a two-car garage it's not practical to park your civilian car in it, however you can, but you'll be moving stuff in and out every time you need to work on the street rod.

"before" my first project a 1930 Ford 2 Door

"after" Presenting key to BETSYS A to my wife Betsy

You can see the garage in the background of the above right picture. I was moving stuff in and out the whole process, but that was OK, I was young and didn't mind.

Yes, you can build your car in a two-car garage. Hopefully your spouse is behind you on this project because once you have all the parts, the body and the chassis at home it will change your life style. We had the laundry room in the garage and still used it as storage for that long time accumulated junk. We parked the cars on the driveway until the street rod was done.

If you have a 3-car garage or a second garage, life will be much simpler.

When we moved from Santa Maria to Moreno Valley we again had a 2-car garage house, but we had a half-acre of property so I built a small 900 sq ft shop next to the house.

STREET
ROD
PARTS

To the left of the house was the shop you see in the picture on the left above and attached to the right side of the house is the garage in the picture on the right above. As you can see, it didn't solve my problem; more garage space equals more street rods. Actually the red '32 on the right was a car waiting delivery to a customer, the purple '29 4-door sedan is Betsy's second BETSYSA. Before I built the shop I built two cars in the attached 2-car garage.

What a difference the shop made. Look, you can build two at a time.

WHAT PARTS DO I NEED TO BUY

The popular street rod magazines have tons of advertisements for street rod parts. Street Scene (NSRA), Street Rodder, Rod and Custom, and Hot Rod are examples. I'm going to give you my favorite sources, which have been developed through experience over the years. Yearwood Speed and Custom www.yearwood.com has a wide variety of stuff for your street rod. Also JC Whitney www.jcwhitney.com has a lot of stuff.

Chassis Parts

I've already discussed chassis and chassis components so we'll look at those parts you need in addition to the complete chassis as it's delivered from the chassis dealers.

Tires and wheels:

I've found that the magazine ads have some of the best prices, but shipping can ruin a good deal, however, most of the time you save on the tax and that nullifies the added shipping cost. I have always found a reasonable resource in my hometown and do all my tire/wheel business there. This item can make or break a street rod. The size and type of tires and wheels are important when planning out your street rod. As an example when I build a hi-boy (no fenders) I like big and littles. That is a big tire on the back and little on the front. For me, ideal is 285/70/15's on 8"-10" rims on the back and 195/60/14's on 6" rims on the front. The new hi-tech rods have like 18"-20" rims and very low profile tires. It's all a matter of preference and the type of rod you're going to build, hi-tech, conventional, or nostalgia. Do some research and make a choice.

Drive train:

Engine: Whatever you want, but keep in mind that the Chevy small block is the least expensive and easiest to maintain. I put a Ford in my wife's '27 Ford coupe and it cost me almost double what a Chevy would've cost and the parts were much harder to find. There are lots of good engine dealers in the street rod magazines, but I would try to find one close to home

I put a Ford in my wife's '27 Ford coupe and it cost me almost double what a Chevy would've cost and the parts were much harder to find.

due to the heavy weight and shipping. Sometimes the dealers can deliver at a competitive price. There's also eBay. You can get an engine fully equipped or short or small block. For all the accessories there are dozens of suppliers in the magazines. I like Jegs the best http://www.jegs.com, PAW http://www.pawengineparts.com, and Summit http://www.summitracing.com are also good. For street rod Jet-Hot coated hugger headers I found Southern Rods www.southernrods.com is the best price. Here is a list of engine parts you need to consider:

Carburetor, intake manifold, air cleaner, distributor, coil, ignition wires, wire looms, exhaust manifold, short water pump, engine & transmission dip-sticks, oil filter, radiator hoses (cool flex is cool), appropriate vacuum hoses for the carburetor, trans, power brake, and distributor. Valve covers, alternator and A/C brackets (Bills Hot Rod Company is my favorite 626-332-1915), alternator, engine mounts (the chassis dealer should have the appropriate engine mounts), and carburetor linkage.

Transmission, mount and torque converter: Most transmission shops have what you want. The Chevy Turbo 350 and 400 are the most popular and the 700R4 is also popular, but more expensive. You're looking at around $500 for a rebuilt Turbo or $1000 for a rebuilt 700R4. This includes a stock torque converter. If you want high RPM torque converter it will cost more. You can get them at a junkyard for around 150-300 bucks, but buyer beware. Even though they give you a warrantee the problems don't show up until months later when you get the car on the road, then you have to spend time removing it to exchange it. I've even had guaranteed trany's from a shop go bad. The same suppliers I mentioned above under engine also carry transmissions. I've never built a car with a stick or convention transmission, but the same resources above carry them. The 5 and 6 speeds are popular now, but really expensive.

Drive shaft: Most cities have a driveline shop and if yours doesn't, the biggest one nearest you will. A drive shaft with u-joint will cost you around $150-$200. There's a measuring technique that varies between shops and they will give you directions.

Radiator: There are lots of radiator manufacturers to choose from. When you order one you need tell them if it will need an A/C coil built into it and let them know what engine you'll be running. My favorite is Walker Radiator Works and you can find the closest supplier at 1-800-821-1970. Griffin Thermal Products (Griffin Radiators) in SC http://griffinrad.com makes a good aluminum, but is a more expensive than the Walker. The Brass Works in San Luis Obispo, CA http://www.thebrassworks.net is another option. US Radiator http://www.usradiator.com in Vernon, CA is popular.

Exhaust: You will have to search around your own community to see if anyone specializes in street rod exhaust systems. Most muffler shops can handle it. When I lived in CA I found a shop in my own town that did both mufflers and wheels and he gave me a discount because I used him for both. Don't be afraid to ask for a discount or a better deal.

Body Parts

If you're building a glass car, the manufacturer who sold you the car will also have the glass parts to go with it. Here's a a list of things you potentially might need; radiator shell, radiator lower apron, hood, inner fenders, fenders, running boards, splash aprons, gas tank cover, bumpers, or a roll pan under the trunk and rear frame horns.

If you're building a metal car, there are vintage car part dealers who sell after market fenders, radiator shells, hoods, inner fenders, running boards, splash aprons, and gas tank covers. CW Moss www.cwmoss.com in Orange, CA and Vintage Ford and Street Rod Parts www.vintageford-streetrod.com in Hunting Beach, CA and Macs Antique Auto Parts www.macsautoparts.com in Lockport, NY are just a few. If you're building something other than a Ford email me and I'll try to help you find what you need. These guys also carry stuff like moldings, trim, door/trunk handles, lights, turn signals, all in original style.

Miscellaneous Parts

There are many items you need to consider for your car such as switches, gauges, instrument panel, gear shift, steering column and wheel, column drop, seat belts, interior light, stereo, seating, air condition, heater, cruise control, wiring, gas tank, head/tail lights, turn signals, horn, gear shift, emergency brake, hood latch mechanism (TCI http://www.totalcostinvolved.com makes a nice inexpensive one), windshield wiper, door handles, window handles, parking brake, trunk opener, battery, battery cables, radiator cooling fan, and license plate holder. Decide on a color and type of paint you want on your car.

There are a number of places you can buy this stuff and I've tried most of them so I'm going to give you a list of some of my favorites. Also your local auto parts carry a lot of this stuff.

Yearwood Speed and Custom (variety) www.yearwood.com
Southern Rods & Parts (variety) www.southernrods.com
JC Whitney (variety) www.jcwhitney.com
Yogi's (variety) www.yogisinc.com
Rod Doors (upholstery panels) www.roddoors.com
EZ Wiring www.ezwiring.com
Dolphin Instruments www.dolphingauges.com
Classis Instruments www.classicinstruments.net
Jaz Products (gas tanks) www.jazproducts.com
Tanks Inc (gas tanks) www.tanksinc.com
Speedway Motors (variety) www.speedwaymotors.com
Tea's Design Seats, Rochester, NY 507-289-0494 for brochure.

Tools

ENGINE HOIST

Hand tools:

A complete set of mechanics hand tools are needed. You probably already have a set of hand tools, but if you don't, I recommend Sears Craftsman www.craftsman.com. There is a Sears in almost every city and they have the best guarantee I've seen. If you break a tool they exchange it for free, no questions asked. One time I found an old Craftsman screwdriver in my back yard. It was rusted beyond repair and when I took it in to Sears, they gave me a new one right on the spot. Sears is always having great sales on their tools and if you belong to their Craftsman Club you save even more. It's a free membership and you can join at the store. Another good source is Snap-on www.snapon.com, but be ready for price shock, their good quality and also have a lifetime guarantee. Harbor Freight www.harborfreight.com has about anything you may want at reasonable prices.

Power tools and equipment:

When I was building my first car I had a few basic power tools, but I learned fast the job is much easier when using the right equipment. For example trying to drill a ¼ in. thick steel bracket with a small hand held electric drill is way harder than using a drill press. You can get your power tools from the same suppliers I listed above. Here's a list of power tools you should consider:

Drill – electric or pneumatic and cordless
Drill press – bench or floor
Drill bit set and hole saw set
Impact wrench - elect or pneumatic
High-speed grinder/cutter – elect or pneumatic
Saber saw
Air compressor
Welder (not a must have, but nice if you can do it)
Metal chop saw
Engine hoist and engine stand
Jack stands 4 each

Basic body working tools:

If you plan on painting the car yourself you will need some basic tools and equipment; an air compressor, paint spray gun, long and short block sanders, sander/polisher, and lots of elbow grease. In addition to the suppliers above Eastwood www.eastwood.com has body work tools.

WOW
REALLY
COOL

CHAPTER 3 - "Time to Act"

ORDER THE STUFF

It's time to start taking action. You've decided on the type of car you want to build, where to get the body, chassis, parts, and tools. Pull out that credit card and call or click on all your suppliers and order all the stuff you need to build your street rod. This is a really hard step because it requires you to spend a lot of money. Figure between 20 and 40K unless you're going to build a "T" bucket, which you can do for around 10 to 20K. If this depresses you, just think what it would cost if one of the "big boys" were building it for you, between 70 and 100K for a basic, nothing fancy rod. For about 40K building it yourself you can build a nice full fender '32 Ford 5 window coupe with all the bells and whistles. You need to be specific when ordering, write down what you want on each order, i.e., Heritage Hot Rods '32 Ford 5 window 3" chopped coupe with power windows installed, electric solenoid door openers installed, electric trunk opener installed, stock dash, radiator shell with grill, fenders, running boards, smooth hood, gas tank cover, splash aprons for radiator and running boards, rear frame horns, and window frames (usually included with body). If you're building a '32 5 window, there's your list. You want the chassis too? OK here it is; Total Cost Involved complete '32 Ford Independent Front Suspension (IFS) chassis with chrome stainless package, set up for Chevy 350 engine, turbo 350 transmission, with a 3.0 polished and chrome Jag rear end, hi-tech polished 4 wheel disk brake setup, stainless brake lines, and rack and pinion steering. Those two lists are the bulk of your investment and depending on how wild you get with the motor, it shouldn't cost you much more to get the rest of the stuff. Have at it!

ORGANIZE THE STUFF

Now that everything is here you need to go through it and put it somewhere out of the way until you're ready for it. As you do this catalog it on a list and give it's location so you can find it easily. I made the mistake of not doing this at first and wasted many hours trying to locate stuff.

> I made the mistake of not doing this at first and wasted many hours trying to locate stuff.

LETS GO TO WORK

454 cubes
TURNED
OUT
REALLY
FAST

Fit the Body to the Frame

The Body

The first thing you need to do is assemble the car. If the chassis isn't already together you need to temporally assemble it and install the tires and wheels on the chassis. Now you have what's referred to as a rolling chassis.

Most dealers deliver the complete chassis assembly together. If not, you will need to temporarily install the front and rear end assemblies to the frame.

It's time to put the body on the frame.
For this step you will need to get some of your buddies to help unless you have a lift attached to the ceiling or have a special "A" frame tall enough to lift the body high enough to clear the chassis while you roll it under the body.

31

Regardless of how you do it, you need to put the body on the frame.

Align the forward mount holes in the body with the forward mount holes in the frame. A new frame will have nut plates pressed into the holes. The mount bolts are usually 3/8 or 7/16. Install the forward mount bolts loosely. Now go rearward to the next set of mount holes and install the bolts. Seldom do the mount holes line up so you will have to ream the hole in the body or oblong it enough to be able to start the mount bolt and use a large heavy washer to cover the hole and ad strength to the attachment. Continue rearward until all the mount bolts are started, and then tighten them.

Doors and Trunk

Install the doors and trunk lid and check their alignment. You can adjust them by loosening the hinges a little and manipulating the door a little then tightening them up. Repeating this until you are satisfied with the alignment. Sometimes you will have to shim the body between the frame and the body. On a glass car where the trunk lid upper or forward edge meets the body edge you will probably have to sand off some of the material on the under side of the trunk lid because they usually rub when opening and closing. As you do this remember that there will be about a 1/16" layer of paint when the car is finished.

> The forward edge of the trunk lid on a glass car usually rubs the body when it is opening and closing.

Fenders Etc.

Now install the rest of the body parts and bolt them together. If it's a glass car you will have to clamp them together, drill holes and insert bolts and nuts. Where the body bolts to the pre-drilled and nut-plated holes in the frame you will have to locate where to drill the holes on the glass parts such as the forward fenders. To do this oil the holes and put some sticky clay in the holes, then push the glass part into position against the sticky clay. Remove the part and the clay should be stuck to the part identifying where the hole needs to be drilled. Drill the holes and bolt together.

Temporally install the radiator and radiator shell and check the fit of the hood and install the hood latch mechanism.

> I've fitted and installed several hoods. It's the hardest part of this whole process and I've never been satisfied with the results. There are people who specialize in hoods and can do it for you, but they are expensive.

If you're running a stock style gas tank that attaches to the back of the frame like a '32 Ford, go ahead and fit it now too.

Window Frames and Dash
Fit the window frames and drill and countersink the mount holes.

The dash should already be fitted and installed when you get the body. Fit the instrument panel where you want it and use it as a template to mark the instrument holes and cut them out with the appropriate hole saw (usually 2 1/8"). The instrument gauges hold the panel in place. Also, drill the holes for the switches and A/C outlets if used. Now the dash and window frames are ready for paint prep and paint.

Steering Column and Brake Pedal (after market car only)

Install the brake pedal and rotate it upward until it hits the floorboard of the car and make a mark with a marker where the top of the brake pedal hits the floorboard. Using a 3" hole saw, cut a hole so the top of the hole is ¼" above the mark and the mark is in the centerline of the hole. Raise the pedal so the head of it goes through the hole and it stops when the pedal body hits the bottom of the hole and mark the floorboard on each side of the pedal body. Now using a saber saw cut a vertical rectangular hole downward 3" long and 1/8" bigger on each side of the 2 marks you just made. The brake pedal should easily have full travel up and down and in and out of the floorboard.

Steering column. Measure 2 ¾" outboard from the side of the brake pedal body on the inside of the floorboard and make a mark. Now measure from the just made mark vertically upward 3" and make an X mark. Using a 2 1/8" hole saw cut a 2 1/8" hole with the X mark at the center. Tape the end of the steering column and with the steering wheel attached, insert it into the 2 1/8" hole and position it where you want. You will probably have to oblong the hole a little. Have someone hold it in place while you attach the column drop loosely to the steering column. There should be a steel cross member just behind the dash. This is where you want to connect the column drop. If there's no cross member, get a 1" square steel tube and weld it onto the steel frame work near the door posts, or have some pre-drilled tabs welded on it and bolt it onto the steel framework. You could attach the column drop to the bottom of the dash, but if the dash is glass, there wouldn't be any strength and it could easily

34

break away. You will probably have to build a steel bracket for attaching the column drop to the cross member. Look at the picture on page 53 (the red car) (click here).

Gas Tank (not the stock type) and Battery

I always use a Jaz Fuel Cell and mount it in the trunk with the battery. They are only about $150 for a 15-gallon tank and easy to work with. I order it so it mounts upright with the fill, feed, vent and sending unit on top. You have to cut a hole to fit the sending unit that came with the gauges. I build a frame out of 2"x1/8" steel angle iron to sit on the floor and hold the tank and battery. I weld it together and mount it against the back of the bulkhead framework and the floor in a way that it sits level. Then use steel or adjustable tie down straps to attach the fuel cell to the upper bulkhead and framework (see the picture below), this makes for easy removal.

That's it for fitting the body.

The Chassis

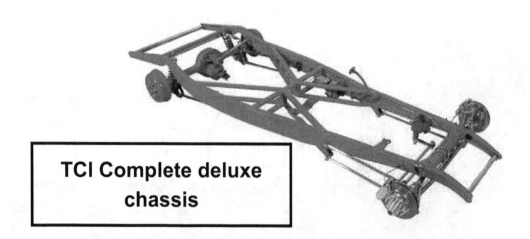

TCI Complete deluxe
chassis

Completely disassemble the chassis while cataloging the parts and keeping them organized for easy access when needed in a couple of days.

If you are building an original car and using the original frame you will need to remove the body from it, sand blast it, box it in and perform the necessary modifications for the suspension and drive train you are going to use. These will probably involving cutting and welding. After the modifications are complete, the process is the same as for new aftermarket chassis.

Take the frame, transmission mount, and brake pedal to your local or nearest powder coater. They will sand blast it and powder coat to the color of your choice. If you're building a non-show full fender driver, I would suggest black because it shows the least dirt and grime and that's important on the underside of the car when you are putting lots of miles on it. While the frame is at the powder coaters paint the rear end the color of you choice.

Set the frame on four jack stands. Make sure you pad the jack stands so you don't scratch the frame.

Depending on the kind of front end you

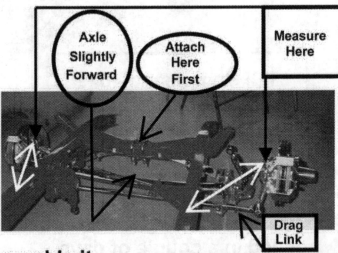

have, you will either have to assemble it (IFS) to the frame or position it (dropped axle as pictured above) with a floor jack under the frame and assemble it to the frame attaching the "U" bolts first. Install the upper parallel bars next and adjust the measurement between the center of the King Pin to the center of the first bolt hole behind the motor mount so that the measurement on both sides are the same, this aligns the axle with your frame. Now install the lower parallel bars and adjust so they are the same length and the lower part of the axle is slightly forward. The drag link adjusts the toe-in toe-out attitude of the wheels. Adjust so that the front center

These adjustments will get you down the road safely and will be close enough to just need fine tuning when you take it to the alignment shop. I've had cars that I drove for years and never had them in an alignment shop. If it rides nice and the tires aren't wearing, you may want to skip the alignment shop.

inside measurement between the front wheels is the same as the back measurement.

Adjust the cams and the lower adjustment rods on the IFS so the wheel sits perpendicular to the ground and adjust the steering rods so the toe-in/toe-out is neutral by measuring the same as above with the dropped axle.

Now position the rear end under the frame with a floor jack and attach the coil-over shocks first. Then attach the 4

A system with 4 parallel bars on the front or the rear is referred to as a 4 bar system. A system with a bar that connects in 2 places on one end and 1 place on the other end is referred to as a hairpin system.

parallel bars to the frame and the rear end mounts while aligning, measuring and adjusting the rear end with the floor jack and adjusting the length of the 4 bars so the rear end sits with the snout in a slight upward pointing position toward the transmission mount. After you have got the rear end attached and adjusted the forward attitude, install the sway bar and adjust the rear end snout so it is centered in the middle of the frame. The 3rd member will be slightly to the left side of the frame and the snout will be centered. If you look close, you can see it in the picture above. If you are

38

using an anti roll bar on the rear end, install it now. The rear end is now finished.

Reinstall the brake lines, master cylinder and brake pedal. Add brake fluid to the master cylinder. I prefer the silicone fluid because it won't eat paint if spilled.
Now you need to bleed the air out of the brake system. Open the bleeder valve on the brake farthest from the master cylinder, the rear passenger brake. If you have disk brakes, always bleed the lower outside cylinder first, then the lower inside one, then the upper outside one and then the upper inside one. Attach a small enough rubber hose that it has a tight fit, to the bleeder valve (valve is already open) and put other end of it in a clear glass or plastic jar. Pump the brake until fluid comes out the rubber hose into the jar. Keep pumping and adding fluid to the master cylinder when necessary until there are no more bubbles coming out the end of the hose. While the hose is still submerged in the fluid tighten the bleeder valve and then remove the hose. Repeat this procedure for the driver rear brake then the passenger front brake and lastly the driver front brake. This needs to be repeated with a second person.

Always bleed the brakes that are the farthest away from the master cylinder first. Most new model master cylinders are duel chamber, front and rear. Do the rear first and then the front.

Set up the same way as above, but don't open the bleeder valve. Have the other person pump up the brake until the pedal stays up and won't compress. Then while the other person maintains pressure on the pedal, open the valve until the brake pedal goes all the way down. Before letting the pedal come back up, close the bleeder valve. Repeat until there are no bubbles in the out going fluid. Follow the same order as before, passenger rear, driver rear, passenger front, and driver front. If you have power brakes, repeat again with the engine running and the power booster vacuum hose hooked up to a vacuum source when able.

Install the tires and wheels and this completes the basic chassis assembly and set up. Tires and wheels should have been balanced during mounting when purchased.

If you're using a stock gas tank that is mounted on the frame like some of the early Fords, paint and install it now.

Register the Car (using your title or the one you bought - page 12)

Get an aluminum plate 1/8" thick ¾" wide and long enough to stamp your vehicle identification number (VIN) on it, drill a 1/8" hole at each end of it and stamp the VIN on the plate between the holes, then pop rivet it onto the frame in a place that is not to hard to view. Now go down to the Dept. of Motor Vehicles (DMV) and get all the forms to re-register a car that is no longer in the system. One of the forms they will give you will be a VIN verification form and can be verified by any policeman. Once you have all the forms call the local police department and tell them you need a VIN verification. They will send a patrolman out to your house (this is a normal occurrence for them). Have the form filled out with the VIN on it but not where the patrolman will fill in his/her information. They might want to see the title so have it handy. All they are doing is verifying the VIN, they're not inspecting your project or looking for smog compliance.

After the patrolman completes the form you can take all the completed forms down to the DMV, pay the fees and that's it. Most DMV's are crowded so get an appointment; it will save you waiting for a couple of hours or more.

WOW!
WHAT'S THE BIG DEAL

The Engine (this section could be done earlier)

If you haven't already, using the engine hoist (pictured at the heading of the Tools section) or another lifting mechanism, put the engine on the engine stand. I'm assuming a Chevy engine is being used, if not, these directions may be changed slightly. Modify the engine as planned and install the parts you ordered except the ones listed below. If you are installing a custom crank case pan, you need to do it first by turning the engine upside down, removing the old pan, clean thoroughly and seal generously with a high temp silicone sealer between the new gasket and the pan. Torque the pan bolts very lightly then let stand for a full day before torqueing to the manufacturers specifications. Chrome pans have a reputation for leaking. This method should prevent any leaks. Remember you can't remove and replace the timing chain cover without removing or lowering the front part of the pan so if you decide to install a chrome or aluminum timing chain cover, do it now.

If you already have the engine while waiting on the other stuff you might as well work on it. No reason to sit idle if you have something you could be doing.

41

The ignition wiring, electrical wiring, hoses, carburetor, air cleaner, distributor, and new valve covers (use old ones for now) install later. You don't want to risk damage to them while installing the engine in the frame.

The Transmission (This could be done earlier also)

Hopefully you got a transmission from a reputable dealer and the only thing you need to do is dress it up. Even buying from a dealer, you can have problems. The difference is that a reputable dealer will stand behind the transmission and fix or replace it if necessary at no charge to you, even if it's in the car. Buying from a private party or a junkyard, you are gambling that it's a good one and I've found that more often than not, they need work. Transmissions are expensive to have worked on and for less money you can buy a rebuilt from a dealer with a warrantee for less money than to have one fixed when it's in the car and you won't know if it's good or bad until you

I've been stung more than once while trying to save money on a transmission and buying one from a junkyard or a private party. You have no recourse when something goes wrong.

drive it. If you want a shift kit in it you should have ordered it that way. If you didn't, take it in and have one put in it before you install it in the car. I've installed a couple of shift kits and even a 700R4 step down modification with success, but I wouldn't recommend it and I wouldn't try it again, I was lucky. Now's the time to install the transmission dress up stuff and transmission mount. If you got a new transmission chrome or aluminum pan and need to install it, put the transmission on an engine stand and turn it up side down.

42

Remove the old pan and clean the pan mounting area thoroughly, seal generously with a high temp silicone sealer between the gasket and the pan. Install the new pan and tighten the pan bolts lightly and let sit for a day and then tighten to the manufacturers specifications.

Install the Engine and Transmission

Lay down some soft material like an old blanket of something on the floor and set the engine on it with a 4x4 wood block under the harmonic balance. This won't hurt the crank or the harmonic balance as most the weight is on the rear of the pan. Install the flywheel and then the torque converter to the back of the crankshaft. With the transmission on a padded floor jack as to not scratch the bottom of the transmission pan, align the shafts rectangular end with the rectangular receptacle inside the back of the torque converter. Now slide the transmission forward into the torque converter until the transmission bell housing snugs up to the back of the engine block and install the mounting bolts.

Raise the front of the chassis about 2-4 inches with the floor jack and put padded jack stands under the frame just behind the 4 bar mounts to hold it up when you let the floor jack down and move it out of the way. Using the engine hoist, lift the engine and transmissions high enough to clear the rolling chassis and with the help of another person, roll the engine and transmission over the chassis until the motor mounts are aligned with the motor mounts on the frame. Lower the engine and transmission and at the same time use the floor jack under

Make sure the transmission mount is not installed. Wait until after the engine mounts are attached to the frame.

the transmission pan to adjust the height of the transmission until the engine mounts are aligned in such a way that the engine mount bolts can be installed. Use 5/16x4½ "high stress" bolts with lock nuts.

Raise transmission with the floor jack until the top of the transmission touches the bottom of the frame. Install the transmission mount. Lower the transmission so the mount is almost touching the frame mount. Align one of the mount-bolt holes with a Phillips screwdriver while inserting and starting the threads on the other bolt. Insert and start the threads on the second bolt. On some transmission mounts there's only one bolt. Tighten bolts. Use 5/16x1½ "high stress" bolts.

Install the transmission cooler on the passenger side of the frame on a cross member so it faces into the air stream under the car. If you're using the radiator to cool the transmission oil, you can hook it up when you install the radiator below. Also install the gearshift and emergency brake if you're using one.

> I prefer to use a trans. cooler rather than the radiator for cooling the transmission oil. It is much cleaner and the lines are back and out of site when looking at the engine.

Finish the Engine

Finish installing the rest of the engine parts and install the radiator and radiator hoses. If you are using the radiator to cool the transmission oil you can run and hook up those lines now. If you're not running a heater, install plugs in the water pump and intake manifold. If you are running a heater, install them anyway until later. Mount the fuel pump on the

(electric fuel pump)

inside passenger side of the frame just above the center of the rear 4 bar, and run the fuel lines to the gas tank with the fuel filter inline close to the gas tank, and the engine. Ground the engine to the frame with a grounding strap.

The Drive Shaft

You will have to have a special drive shaft made connecting a GM transmission to a Ford rear end. Most driveline shops can do this. You can get an aluminum (polished later if you like) or a standard steel drive shaft. There are a couple of measurements you will need; the distance from back of the rear housing to the center of the rear u-joint cup holder; and the measurement of the diameter of the cup holder. Also, you need the year, make and model of the transmission. After you receive the drive shaft, install it.

Service the Fluids

Before you forget, you need to service the fluids. This will prevent you from forgetting whether you serviced them or not and show you where there are leaks if any. The brakes are already serviced so all you need to do is service the rear end oil (usually 3 pints of SAE 90W), transmission oil (Usually about 11 quarts of Dextron III), and the engine oil (5 quarts, your preference). The wheel bearings are supposed to have been lubed at the supplier, but it doesn't hurt to check. All the ball joints need to be lubed. The u-joints are usually lubed at the driveline shop; you'll know when you install the drive shaft. Also, service the radiator with antifreeze.

Test Run the Engine

Now would be a good time for testing the engine and fine-tune the timing and the carburetor and power bleeding the brakes.

Roll the chassis out onto the driveway and set a gas container with gas in it below and near the rear end with a hose going to the inlet of the fuel pump.

Set the battery to the passenger side of the frame just outboard of the starter motor and wire it to the starter motor solenoid battery terminal, ignition system, and the fuel pump. Then ground the battery to the frame. Use a remote starter cord hooked up to the starter and the battery.

Wearing hear protection, start the engine, fine tune it and bleed the brakes with the help of a second person.

You could take the chassis down the muffler shop and this point and have the exhaust system done or you could wait until the car is drivable.

CHAPTER - 4 Work the Body

Notice the piano dolly

BODYWORK, PREP PAINT AND PAINT

The chassis is finished so you need to focus on the body now. Who's going to do the body? You or will you have it done. There's no shame in having your paint and upholstery done. That's probably the most nit-picked item on a street rod so its understandable if you want to have it done right.

There are a lot of good body and paint shops that will give you a great job for a reasonable price. Do some research in your town and find one of them. At the cost of the new paints, you can have it done for not that much more.

Having a Body and Paint Shop Do It

Shop around your area for a good body shop that will do the job for a reasonable price. Most shops mix their own paint so they can be competitive. Take in your brake pedal so they can do an exact match to the color of your frame. Like I said before, you should be able to get a good job for between $1000 and $2000 depending on what you have i.e., full fenders, hood, splash aprons, etc.

> While the body shop is working your body you could be working the dashboard and inside window frames. If you want the same color on the dash and window frames as what's going on the car, you need to take them into the body shop also. Or, you can have the shop do it all.

Doing the Body Yourself

The first thing you need to do with your glass body is to sand off all the seams on the body and body parts. If you are doing an original metal car you have to strip off all the old paint and treat the metal with a corrosion preventative.

Now spray on a couple of thick coats of primer surfacer, let it dry completely (refer to the directions on paint can), and then block sand the body and body parts with 100-grit paper. Remove the dash to work it. This will show you where all the small dents and dimples are located. Using body filler on the deeper dents and glazing compound on the shallow dents, apply to the body and parts. Let it completely dry and block sand it with-100 grit until it's smooth with the rest of the surface.

Spray another thick coat of primer surfacer on the body and parts and block sand it again. If there are still dimples or dents, repeat the body filler/glazing compound process. Repeat this until the body is free of dents and dimples, then spray on one last thick coat of primer surfacer and hand sand the entire surface of the body and parts with 320 grit paper until there is no sand marks and the surface is smooth as glass. Now you can paint the color coat:

Wipe down the surface with a tack cloth (a soft sticky cloth used for picking up dust) and paint several light coats. Let it dry and then apply another several coats and repeat this process until the color coat is to your satisfaction and let completely dry for a day or so.

> If you get dust or insects or imperfections in the paint, between coats you can wet sand them out with 400 grit wet/dry/paper and water. You need to be very light and careful doing this because the paint will be soft and can easily be torn.

Now you need to wet-sand all the surfaces with a 400 grit wet/dry paper and water. When all the surfaces are smooth and clear of sand marks and imperfections you will be ready for the clear coat. As before with the color coat, apply the clear coat lightly until you have a nice shiny surface. You can put on as many coats as you like, but not all at once or it will run.

Let the paint completely dry for a week or so and then wet sand it with an 800-1000 grit wet/dry paper and water. When the surface is smooth and clear wet sand it again with an ultra fine 1400-2000 grit paper. Now use an ultra fine polishing compound and the sander/polisher at low speed with a polishing attachment. Be careful, you can easily polish right through the paint.

Next use a glazing cream with the polisher or by hand and you will see a shine like you've never imagined. This is the point where you will realize it was all worth it, Wow! OK, now you need to protect it with a good wax finish like McGuire's Yellow Wax.

CHAPTER - 5 Assemble Car

MOUNT THE BODY

Front Fenders and Running Boards

If you're running fenders and running boards, you need to mount the front fenders and running boards now before you mount the body. Install the front fender braces and running board braces to the frame. Glue some 2" body welting to the frame where the body will contact the frame. Cut out areas around the body to frame mount boltholes. Attach the front fenders to the splash aprons and running boards with ¼" nuts and bolts.

If you're running a hi-boy (no fenders) just disregard the direction referring to the fenders.

With one or two helpers, bolt the fenders and splash aprons to the frame and the running boards to the running board braces.

The Body and Rear Fenders

With the help of several people pick up the body and gently set it in place on the frame and bolt it down. To bolt on the rear fenders you will have to jack up the rear with the floor jack under the rear end using a pad to protect the paint and remove the rear tires and wheels. Now you can bolt on the rear fenders. The doors and trunk lid will not go on at this point.

CHAPTER 6 - Wire the car

WIRE THE DASH

You can buy wiring harnesses for the dash, but they are expensive. I personally like wiring it myself. You'll need a variety of colors in 16-gauge wire and a supply of crimp type connectors. You can buy a pretty good connector kit at the local electronic supply store or one of the local hardware stores such as Home Depot or Ace Hardware. You'll also need 2 or 3 (10-wire), male-female connector joints. This will enable you to easily remove the dash without having to unhook a bunch of wires. Install the instrument panel and all the gauges and switches in the dash. Turn the dash up side down. Draw a picture of the back of the dash as you see it now indicating each gauge and switch by name. If you have turn signals the right is now on the left. Don't ask me why I easily remember to pass this on to you. As you wire keep in mind they have to be long enough to reach the wire joint connector and far away enough to hide up in the upper dash area. You can run all the instruments with a positive connection (+) in series from one to the other to the fuse panel. Do the same with the ground connection (-), one to the other and then to a ground source such as one of the steel cross-members. Now run the rest of the individual wires to the instruments i.e., fuel, oil, temperature, and speedometer. If you're using turn-signal

> This is one of my favorite tasks. I've wired many a dash on the dining room table. I like to take my time and enjoy working in the house for a change.

indicators they will have a ground wire and feed from the steering column. The headlight switch usually has it's own fuse and should be wired directly to the headlights, tail lights, dome light, and instrument lights. I like putting in a radiator fan switch also, so I can control the fan. This is a simple on/off switch with a hot wire feed and then out to the fan. The fan grounds to the engine. The ignition switch will have a 10-gage wire 12 volt feed directly from the battery or the battery terminal on the starter solenoid. It will have an ignition feed wire going to the coil or distributor and a feed wire going to the start post of the starter solenoid, a 12-volt feed and an accessory feed going to the fuse block. If you have A/C and/or heat, that needs to be wired into the dash or to the dash also.

> It's very important to identify each wire with tape and when you insert them into the joint connectors to draw a picture of which wire is in which hole of the connector.

Be sure to use wire ties to tie all the wires together in a nice neat configuration. You're now ready to wire the car.

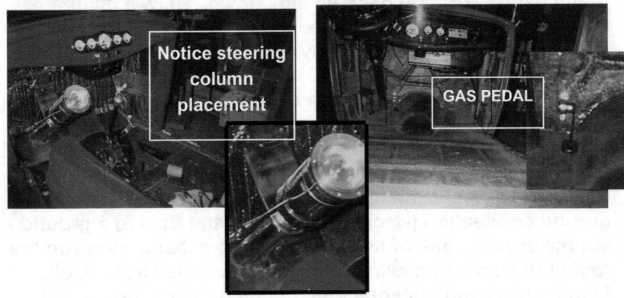

Notice steering column placement

GAS PEDAL

53

Wires going to the engine bay

Here are before and after pictures of what wiring looks like before you wire tie, and after. This was without an aftermarket harness. Also notice the steering column and how it attaches and upright it is. I built this car for a guy in a wheel chair. Enlarge the picture to see closer.

WIRE THE BODY

At this point the dash and steering column have not been installed yet. Don't install them until later, they will be in the way. You can wire the body the old fashioned way, from point a to point b, one at a time, like I did in the picture above or you can use one of the aftermarket wiring kits with the fuse block and all the wires pre-marked and color coded or all one color. Lay all the wire out starting at the fuse block and dash area. All the wires that go to the dash and steering column should go into a joint connector corresponding to the wires on the other end of the joint connector where you marked them. The best way to run the wires is under the side panels and between the carpet padding under the carpet. Run the

It's quite satisfying after wiring the whole car and neatening it up when you turn the key and everything works like it's supposed to.

54

speaker wire if you're using a stereo. The wires going to the engine bay should go through a hole in the lower corner area of the passenger side at the bottom of the firewall area. The wires going to the headlights and turn signals should go forward on the inside of the passenger side of the frame and across the front cross member to the drivers side. Where and how you mount the turn signals and headlights depends on the application and your preference. The engine wires can travel up the back of the engine near the transmission dipstick and up the passenger side of the intake manifold valley. You can get trick and hide the wires in the frame.

"Isn't This Fun"

CHAPTER 7 - Finish the interior

UPHOLSTERY (having it done at a shop)

If you're going to do the interior yourself we'll cover that in the next section.

Install the seat, dash and steering column. Hook up the wiring joint connectors. Install the gas pedal and gas pedal linkage/cable. With some helpers, install the doors and trunk lid. Hook up the door wiring for solenoids and window switches or install the door and window handles. Install the trunk opening mechanism. Install the lights and turn signals. Install the stereo and speakers if you're using one. You can buy a radio box from Dan Fink www.hotrodproducts.com and leave the speakers on the floor, the upholstery shop will

55

mount them somewhere. Put the window frames in the car, the upholstery shop will need them.

Your car is now drivable. Usually the upholsterer will have some good ideas of how to do your interior if you don't. You will spend some time with the upholsterer working it out. Tell him you want an insulator material against the inside skin of the body. Certain carpet pads are protected with a metal foil like substance. Your car could be in the shop for a long time, don't make the mistake of saying, "take your time". I waited 6 months once. Always let them know you're in a hurry.

WINDOWS and MUFFLERS

Find a glass shop that can do your windows. Don't attempt to do them yourself unless you're a professional. Some regular glass shops can do cars so look around, however, the auto glass shops will presumably do a good job and do it right.

If you already haven't done it, you might want to detour to the muffler shop and have the exhaust done. It's been my experience that you can get the exhaust done with aluminized pipe for $300 to $500.

WAS IT WORTH IT
OR WHAT?

That's it you're done (except for the checkout and adjustments), unless you're doing the upholstery yourself and if so I'll see you next section.

UPHOLSTERY (doing it yourself)

Gee! After reading that last section I almost feel like taking the car into the upholstery shop and having it done. However, I don't have that kind of money or I just want to say I did it myself.

LOOK AT THESE BEFORE YOU DECIDE

I did all these interiors for $600-$1200 and I'm in no way an upholstery professional. "INTERESTED", read on.

Remember, the doors, trunk lid, steering column and dash are not installed yet. It's much easier to do the upholstery without the seats, steering column, and doors installed.

In the pictures above the door panels are from Rod Doors and the seats are from Tea's Design Seats. The door panels are plastic and you cut them to fit the doors and attach them with Velcro. The seats come already upholstered and I order 8 yards of matching material to do the door panels, headliner, side panels, kick panels, rear panel, the under dash panel, and the trunk panels. You can also get the matching carpet from Tea's. The seats are about $800 for the bench seat and $1100 for the buckets (remember they come already upholstered).   Rod Doors also sells seats and upholstery materials and accessories for about the same price as Tea's. You can get bucket seats from the junkyard for $100-$300 and have them upholstered for about $300 (might as well by Tea's or Rod Doors). Glide Seats www.glideengineering.com is another option who makes a great seat. Also, I like to use an insulator glued on the inside of the body skin and insulated carpet pad.

Carpet

What do I need? Most big cities have upholstery supply businesses and you can get your materials quite a bit cheaper than upholstery shops. Of course if you buy one of the pre-made upholstered seats you ought to get the matching materials to go with the seats. You also need to get carpet padding for under the carpet and liquid nails to glue it and the carpet down. Use upholstery cardboard panels for the side panels, they come as a 4'x4' sheet, regular or water proof (water proof are thick and hard to cut and work with), you will need 8 of them. Wind lace for the door openings can be made at the upholstery shop out of the material you have for the interior. If you're lucky, the upholstery supply may have some pre-made wind lace in your material.

Make a hole and cover in the floor for master cylinder servicing

Install the carpet. Measure the floor of the car and the trunk and cut out a piece of padding and carpet to cover the area. Now cut and fit the pad and make holes for the seat mount bolts, gear shift, steering column, brake pedal, and gas pedal, then cut the pad inboard of the passenger door about 1½". This is where the wire harness you made will run to the back of the car to the speakers, fuel tank, lights, etc. Glue the pad in place with Liquid Nails. After the glue is completely dry, lay the carpet in place. You will cut 3 pieces, one for the flat part of the floor, one for the tunnel cover, and one for the firewall. Cut the tunnel cover so it overlaps the other two pieces, as they will cover the edges. Cut holes for the seat mounts, gearshift, steering column, brake pedal, and gas pedal. Take the carpet down to the local upholstery shop and have them sew a binding around the exposed edges of the carpet. Now glue the carpet in place starting with the tunnel cover, then the floor piece and then the firewall.

Headliner

Most aftermarket bodies have wooden tack strips for the headliner to mount to. Some cars and originals will have bows. Measure the distance from the forward header where the headliner will attach, to the rear of the tack strip or bow just rearward of it and then measure each bow or tack strip from there rearward to the rear header where it will attach. Now take the measurements and headliner material down to the upholstery shop and have them sew in the seams and tack strips or bow tubes. Next take the headliner and staple the first tack strip to the first wood tack strip rear of the forward header with a staple gun, or slide the bow through the bow tube strip. Now fasten the headliner to the forward header taughting the material between the first tack strip and the header with a staple gun if wood or glue if not. Next staple or bow the remaining tack strips taught as you go until you finish by attaching to the rear header. If you have wood side strips staple the headliner sides to them also in a taught manner.

Door and side panels

Cut the door and side panels to fit. There's a separate panel for each of the front kick panels, posts between the windshield and door, header cover, posts between the door and rear window (if there are rear side windows), rear bulkhead panel, lower side panels under rear side windows or rear lower kick panels (if there are no rear side windows), rear window panel, (surrounds the rear window like a frame), rear upper corner panels, above the door and rear side windows (if any) panels, and the door panels. Look close at the pictures on page 58 and you can see the layout. Cut the window crank and door handle holes if you are using them and any other holes you may need such as speaker outlet holes, etc. The speakers themselves should be mounted to the framework.

Hopefully you're using Rod Doors panels. They already have your design and all you have to do is glue on the material. If not take all the panels that you want a design in down to the upholstery shop and have them sew in the design and finish the panels (this usually is just the door panels and maybe the front kick panels and rear side panels). Then the panels that are plain you will glue the material to them. Practice with some cardboard and cheap throw away material until you get the technique. The corners are the trick.

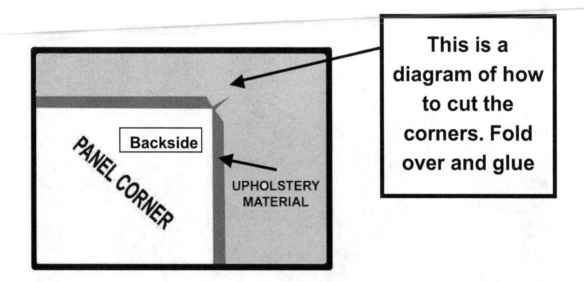

Install the wind lace around the edge of the door opening.
Either glue it to the metal frame or staple it to the wood trim.
Now install the dash and hook up the wire connectors.

OK, now you can install all the panels in the order I listed
them above (except the door panels, You'll install them later).
You may need to make some trim to go in front of the dash
between it and the windshield. Sometimes wind lace works
good.

Doors, Trunk Lid and Steering Column

Install the steering column, steering wheel and accessories,
then attach the doors and install the door panels. Now install
the trunk lid and opener.

WAS IT WORTH
IT OR WHAT?

That's it you're done (except for the checkout and adjustments).

CHAPTER 8 - Checkout & Adjustment

DRIVE THE CAR

Drive the car! Put some miles on it. You are going to find some bugs. Nothing is perfect. Take you tools with you, many times I had to call my wife to bring my tools so don't venture to far from home. There will be leaks, weird sounds and rattles. Vibrations or steer wheel chatter or shimmy. The engine may heat up or the rear end makes noise. One time I exchanged 3 rear ends with Currie before I got one that didn't make noise, even the new ones aren't necessarily right. Obviously all these things won't happen, what I'm saying is to expect them and you won't be caught off guard. Actually I've had many first time rides without a problem.

ADJUSTMENT

There are lots of things to adjust. The brakes may need adjustment if you have drum brakes. You need to bleed them again to get the excess air out of them after a few miles. The steering will probably need adjustment, eventually you will want to take it to an alignment shop and have it fine-tuned. The steer wheel will have to be centered for when you are going in a strait line. Carburetor and engine timing will need to be fine tuned especially if you have a high tech system.

64

Tires and wheels may need fine tuning on the balancer. The sound of the exhaust may not be to your liking. The doors, hood, and trunk may need adjusting after a few miles.

FINISHED AT LAST!

Eventually you'll feel comfortable that everything is OK and ready for the first trip. Even so, take some tools, there's always the unexpected. You should get many years of enjoyment out of your car and when you're ready to sell it, you'll make some money, unless of course "YOU HAD SOMEONE ELSE BUILD IT"!

THE END

LINKS

Brass Works http://www.thebrassworks.net 800-342-6759

Brookville Roadsters http://www.brookville-roadster.com 937-833-4605

Classis Instruments www.classicinstruments.net 800-575-0461

CW Moss www.cwmoss.com 800-322-1932

Dan Fink www.hotrodproducts.com 714-841-6200

Dolphin Instruments www.dolphingauges.com 386-437-1077

Down's Manufacturing http://www.downsmfg.com 269-624-4081

Eastwood www.eastwood.com 800-343-9353

EZ Wiring www.ezwiring.com 386-437-1077

Glide Seats www.glideengineering.com 800-301-3334

Griffin Thermal Products http://griffinrad.com 800-722-3723

Harbor Freight www.harborfreight.com 843-676-2603

Hemmings Motor News http://www.hemmings.com
800-227-4373 ex 550

Heritage Hot Rods http://www.heritagehotrods.com 815-933-7373

Hot Rods Horsepower
http://www.hotrodsandhorsepower.com 203-481-1932

Jaz Products www.jazproducts.com 800-525-8133

JC Whitney www.jcwhitney.com 800-603-4383

Jegs http://www.jegs.com, 800-345-4545

Macs Antique Auto Parts www.macsautoparts.com 800-777-0948

PAW http://www.pawengineparts.com 818-678-3000

Poly Form Fiberglass http://www.poli-form.com 831-722-4418

Radiator Works 800-821-1970

Redneck Strt Rds http://www.redneckstreetrods.com 913-367-8346

Rodbods http://www.rodbodsusa.com 775-358-1930

Rod Doors www.roddoors.com 800-428-7114

Sears Craftsman www.craftsman.com 800-349-4358

Snap-on www.snapon.com 877-762-7664

SO-CAL Speed Shop's http://so-calspeedshop.com 909-469-6171

Southern Rods www.southernrods.com 800-787-8763

Speedway Motors www.speedwaymotors.com 800-979-0122

Steve's Auto Restorations 503-665-2222.
Street Scene magazine http://www.nsra-usa.com 901-452-4030
Summit http://www.summitracing.com 800-230-3030
Tanks Inc www.tanksinc.com 320-558-6882
TCI (Total Cost Involved)
http://www.totalcostinvolved.com 800-984.6259
Tea's Design Seats, 507-289-0494
The Rod Factory http://www.rodfactory.com 602-269-0031
US Radiator http://www.usradiator.com 323-826-0965
Vintage Ford and Street Rod Parts www.vintageford-streetrod.com 714-965-7600
Wescott's Auto http://www.wescottsauto.com 800-523-6279
Woodsy's Gearhead City http://gearheadcity.com 217-684-2400
Yearwood Speed and Custom www.yearwood.com 800-444-3331
Yogi's www.yogisinc.com 800-373-1937
Zig's Street Rods
http://www.zigsstreetrods.com/zigs.html 800-288-7260

PICTURE GALLERY

These are some of the cars I built over the years

Betsy with the first Betsy's A, my first project

BETSYS SECOND BETSYSA

This BETSY'S "T"
her present car

CPSIA information can be obtained
at www.ICGtesting.com
Printed in the USA
LVHW020945261022
731536LV00008B/651